LIZ WATERLAND

READ WITH ME

An Apprenticeship Approach
to Reading

THE THIMBLE PRESS

CONTENTS

My thanks to Clive Davies, headteacher of Northborough School in Peterborough, for the opportunity of first developing the ideas described here; to
Ann Allsopp, for encouraging me to carry on the
work at Brewster Avenue Infants School, Peterborough; and to all the children, their parents, and
my colleagues in several Peterborough schools who
·now use the apprenticeship approach to reading.

L.W.

Printed in Great Britain for
The Thimble Press
Lockwood, Station Road
South Woodchester, Stroud, Glos.
by Short Run Press, Exeter
First published July 1985
Reprinted August 1985
Reprinted January 1986

ISBN 0 903355 17 5

1 There must be a better way . . .

Schools should be good at teaching reading. The subject has had more pages of print devoted to it than any other aspect of primary education. The entire population of Britain should by now be fluent readers, fully aware that books are life-enhancing and personality-developing, eager to read and to be caught up in the printed word.

Patently this is not so. Many people learn to read, more or less efficiently; very few become readers.

After many years of primary teaching and parenting I began, some three years ago, to question my failure to achieve the results I believed to be so desirable. Why are so many children failed or reluctant readers, sometimes within a year of starting school? So much energy and expertise, so many resources have been poured into the teaching of reading; so many children give up the effort as soon as they possibly can. Is reading really a pointless, difficult occupation, or is there something in the way we teach that makes it seem like that to so many people?

In the main the failures I sense in the children in our schools are not quantitative, although there are some very poor readers; most have reading ages reasonably near their chronological ages, a few have excellent scores, two or three years above. The problem is, rather, the qualitative one of children who by objective criteria can read but who in practice seldom do, or who read poorly, stumblingly, without apparently realizing that they are supposed to be making sense.

The easiest way of making clear these sorts of problems (which many teachers and parents will recognize) is to offer, from my own thirteen years' experience, some examples of children who caused me much concern.

The first were perhaps the victims of the texts I had been offering. There was, for instance, Steven. He was ten and scored 13.2 on the Daniels and Diack Test 12. One of the school's successes, one might think. And yet he said, 'I don't read anything much. It's boring, reading.'

There were children like seven-year-old Kim, who kept asking, 'What's this word?' She wouldn't or couldn't use her phonics, which had been painstakingly taught, and couldn't seem to get the idea of making sense out of her reading. She would cheerfully read 'Simon and Elizabeth are having tea in their horse' or 'I was a lorry'. Children like this don't seem to listen to what they are reading, don't in fact seem to have any expectation that written language has meaning. Kim had a reading age of 7.5, a satisfactory score.

Some children reacted to reading sessions with indifference. Andrew, for example, never took his book home; in 'quiet reading time' he whispered and giggled, or flicked idly through his book. When he or children like him read to an adult they sigh and fidget and say after every page, 'Can I stop there?' Andrew's reading age was a year above his chronological age of 8.6.

The occasional child was not content to be so passive in his resistance. Six-year-old Simon once hurled his reading book across the classroom. 'I don't care what happens to them, and I couldn't read it if I did,' he said. (Since he was reading about 'The Happy Trio' at the time, I had some sympathy with the feeling, if not its manifestation.)

Sometimes I came across a child who obviously had absolutely no idea of what reading is at all. Matthew was one who, faced with the Daniels and Diack question cards, 'read' Billy Blue Hat for every card. Did he really believe that all print said Billy Blue Hat? His perfect confidence suggested that he did.

There were also the victims of the straight-line organization we impose with a reading scheme. Simon was one such: at six he was reading, quite reasonably, at orange level. But he believed he was a non-reader. 'I can't read yet,' he said to me. 'I'm only on orange.' When he got to black books, he felt he might be able to read.

At the other extreme was Alison, who kept pestering for a 'real' storybook, a library book; but she was only on *Link-up 3* and not very fluent at that. How could she tackle a library book? I had to say 'Wait till you can read a little more, my poppet.' What I felt I was saying was, 'Wait till you have read more boring books, then you can read the good ones.' It was not the impression I wanted to give about reading.

Last of all came a whole army of children who read well enough; we do not worry about children like them; they hop along from book to book; they quite enjoy reading. These are the average children in most primary schools and are recognizable in one of two ways. First, they exhibit no noticeable reaction to the texts they read, especially if they have no choice of text; they make no comment on the content or characters – in some cases they cannot even remember if they have read Book 5 or not. Second, when such children are offered a choice, they will choose either a book with the shortest, easiest text or one with the brightest cover and pictures. For them the content is, on the whole, immaterial.

There are probably thousands of children like this. They can cope at a functional level with the reading required of them at school and have average test scores. But they are not readers; that is, they have little feeling of pleasure in reading and seldom undertake the activity from choice. Such children do not care about books in any deep sense; for them, reading is not a meaningful occupation.

Here were children full of life and language who loved stories and rhymes and games, and yet somehow I was not offering experiences which would enable such oral energy, such potential, to feed the written word and be fed from it. Why could these children not read or write as they spoke, with as much interest and enthusiasm?

By contrast, there were also children who became fluent, voracious, loving readers. One often hears teachers call them, jokingly, the in-spite-of children: those who will learn no matter what we do. Sometimes they are described, more seriously, as natural readers who need virtually no formal teaching.

What makes these children so successful? What creates the paradoxical situation in which the most successful readers are those we give least instruction to? Is talking about the in-spite-of children quite the joke we think it is?

Somewhere there was a failure. But where, and what to do about it? All the vast quantity of time, effort and resources should have produced something better – especially for beginning readers, for here are laid the foundations of success or mediocrity or failure. The more I examined the foundations I was laying, the shakier they seemed. I wanted children's reading to be fluent, full of meaning and response. I had believed, or behaved as if I believed, that somehow this goal could only be achieved later, when the children were older – when they had 'finished' learning to read – or only by the most able young child, the rare exception.

My attitude to the children I taught was that they knew nothing about reading and I knew everything. I was, as I believe many teachers are, a proponent of the 'feeding the cuckoo' theory of teaching. In this theory the teacher is seen as the parent sparrow flying endlessly back and forth to drop larvae of learning into the beak of the passive and dependent cuckoo chick. Eventually the feeding will have been sufficient and the cuckoo will fly off and fend for itself. The teaching of reading lends itself particularly to this model of education: the chick's diet consists of morsels called 'Book One', 'Supplementary Book 3' or 'word attack skills'; it no longer needs feeding when it can fly unaided into the forests of 'real' books, 'library books' or 'free readers'.

Increasingly, however, I had come to feel that too many of our chicks flew poorly or not at all. The model no longer seemed adequate.

It was this knowledge of failure, this realization that, however important teachers may feel books to be, most children will never enjoy reading enough to do it voluntarily, even as adults, that forced me to reassess all that I had ever believed about teaching reading. It seemed to me that I was approaching reading as if it bore no relation to the rest of the educational process. My philosophy of teaching, as for many teachers, especially in infants schools, is child-centred, seeing education as being based on the needs of the individual child. The school offers children a wide range of experiences and guides them, in a supportive environment, to develop at their own pace according to their needs. Except, and here was the shock, except in reading. In my major interest (the major interest of most infants teachers) I was furthest away from what I believe education to be. I did not 'feed the cuckoo' with science, maths, environmental studies or art. Why did I do so in reading? Does reading demand to be taught differently from everything else that children learn both in school and at home? It was hard to believe that this could be so.

I came to adopt, instead, a view of the learner not as passive and dependent like the cuckoo chick but rather as an active and already partly competent sharer in the task of learning to read. Here the model is apprenticeship to a craftsman (what is, in engineering circles, called 'sitting with Nelly'). Consider the way apprenticeship works: the learner first undertakes the simplest parts of the job, then gradually more complex ones, increasing the share he can cope with and all the time working alongside, under the control of and with the help of, the craftsman. The apprentice does not sit passively with his mouth open; he works actively with the tools of his trade in his hand. (This is, I suggest, what 'learning to read by reading' really means.)

After all, how do little children learn everything they do before school; to speak, to play, even to walk or eat? By living in the real world, wanting to join it, to achieve its competences; and having adults as their models and supports. By trial and error, by correcting their own mistakes, they come closer and closer to the skills they see around them. But none of these skills has been 'taught' in the way that schools understand the word. Children have learned them by wanting to be talkers or walkers, by seeing and gradually understanding talking or walking and by trying to do it too, getting better as their physical and mental dexterity increases.

Perhaps this is how 'natural' readers achieve their success? Could schools also use this approach to make children into readers? It was an enticing thought. But on what basis, and how, can it be done?

In the following pages some answers to those two questions are offered to any adult who feels, as I do, that there must be better ways and better reasons for children to learn to read than those conventionally offered in schools. The theoretical basis for the apprenticeship approach is briefly outlined, and suggestions are made about how such learning might be allowed to happen in the classroom as it does in the real world.

2 Outlining the Theory

Once, like many infants teachers, I considered I knew how to teach reading. I had taught many children the mechanics of the skill; had kept up to date, in a broad sense, with developments; had instituted colour coding in two schools, throwing out *Happy Trio* and *Janet and John* in favour of *Link-Up*, *360* and *One, Two, Three and Away*, and could provide a list of word attack skills and the apparatus to teach them. But I knew little about the theories; I was, to be honest, one of those teachers who had believed that a year's practice was worth ten years' theory. Now I had come to doubt that position. The practice had been less successful than I had believed. The problem was that I was in a position of great weakness: I did not really understand what I, and the children, were doing – or, rather, were trying to do.

But classroom practice should always have a firm and respectable intellectual basis. We cannot any longer – if we ever really could – offer only feelings or instincts or experience as our rationale. This is especially true if we are changing established practice. What will be our justification? Is what we are planning better only in our opinion or can we find support from outside authorities? Any change should deepen and enlarge our understanding of children, reading and teaching. I would urge any teacher, whether committed to change at present or not, to read and consider the evidence offered by language and learning theorists to suggest how and why small children learn.

It would be hard to describe the shock and excitement that I felt when I began to examine the theorists of the apprenticeship approach to beginning reading. For a long time any reading I had done on the topic had been confined largely to practical information – books by John Hughes or Donald Moyle – or to general descriptions of current practice, such as *Extending Beginning Reading* or D.E.S. reports. For the first time I began to want to examine underlying assumptions. With the help of Mrs Byrne at the Peterborough Educational Development Centre Library I began a programme of reading: Edmund Huey, Frank Smith, the Goodmans, Sylvia Ashton-Warner and Margaret Meek. Their writing expressed exactly what I knew reading should be and, what was more, what should be the way of undertaking the teaching of it.

The conventional approach

It became obvious that both my training and my practice had instilled in me, as in many teachers, a view of reading that was almost entirely behaviourist. Reading was viewed as a hierarchy of specific skills, a taxonomy of behaviours, which, if taught in small enough units, one upon the other, with rewards for each demonstration of success, could be built up into a total edifice of reading ability. (At its most extreme this view can be seen in publications like *Alpha and Omega*, which offers virtually a programmed learning package, but in which there is no suggestion that the reading of books might be part of the purpose of that learning.)

This approach – advocated by many theorists and confirmed in the manuals of countless reading schemes – suggests that reading is acquired by strictly logical means for strictly logical purposes and, almost entirely, by formal, sequential teaching. Previous experience with storybooks at home is not credited as being 'reading' although it may be allowed as pre-reading activity.

The characteristics of this approach in the classroom are, usually, a belief in the need for progressively increasing difficulty of text (flash cards, then pre-primers, then Books 1, 2 and 3; or a more flexible version, a colour-coded system); the requirement that children should read virtually every word in their book correctly before going on to a harder one (if they fail they may either repeat the book or be put on a parallel scheme's book at the same level of difficulty), and a firmly structured programme of reading-readiness activities, phonics and word building. Children demonstrate their progress through these skills by moving through the reading scheme, by their ability to perform each succeeding skill without help, and by their scores on a standard reading test (which is often the Schonell word recognition test).

This is, broadly, the way thousands of children learn to read and, by its own criteria, it is often successful. Many children *do* progress from skill to skill fairly satisfactorily and return average scores on reading tests.

The apprenticeship approach

Another view of the reading process, however, questions in its theories what I was questioning in practice. Ronald Morris said in 1970: ' . . . as teachers of reading we are not in business simply to ensure that our children acquire a decent level of reading skill. We are also vitally interested in finding ways of teaching that will ensure that what has been learnt is likely to be put to some profitable use'. This suggests that something more than the ability to read words is needed and by implication suggests an approach that teaches more than the ability to read words. Vygotsky goes so far as to say that the problem facing a beginning reader is not 'mechanical obstacles' but the abstract nature of written language; make written language meaningful and the mechanics will not present such stumbling blocks as they often do.

The major proponents of an alternative view of the reading process are Frank Smith and Kenneth Goodman. They show that, far from being a right/wrong, word-by-word activity, reading is 'a selective process. It involves *partial* use of available *minimal* language cues *selected* from perceptual input on the basis of the reader's *expectations*' (Goodman, 1967). I have italicized what seem to me to be the key words, which differentiate this psycho-linguistic approach from a more behaviourist view. Words like 'partial' and 'minimal' suggest that we are no longer considering an exact science in which every component is equally important to every reader. To encapsulate the difference in a sentence: the behaviourist approach sees the reader as *operated* on by the demands of the text and made to respond by the requirements of what is actually on the page; the apprenticeship model sees the reader as *operating* on the text. The contrast is confirmed by words like 'selected' and 'expectations'. The reader will bring as much to the text as the text brings to the reader.

This is a view of the reading process as a continual interaction between the reader's language experience, understanding of the world and strategies of decoding, and the text's meaningfulness, graphic clues, predictability and interest level. The reader reads a text by making informed guesses as to the likelihood of what that text will mean. These guesses are informed, not by exact knowledge of every word on the page or by insistence on correct interpretation of 'sounds' but by natural-language clues based on the reader's understanding of how language works, which combine to suggest the total meaning.

The implication for teaching is inescapable. Instead of assuming that children can only read what they have been taught, we must assume that they can only read what they understand and can interact with, and that the teaching of words has little influence on this process. Rather, teachers 'must help them to select the most productive clues, to use their knowledge of language structure, to draw on their experiences and concepts' (Goodman). Children should be allowed to behave like apprentices – to be active partners in the task with the adult leading, not driving.

Five Propositions

As we think more about this model of reading, five basic points emerge. Once understood, they offer the teacher a refreshed view of the task that beginning readers undertake.

First, and most important, is the proposition that *in many ways the acquisition of written language is comparable with that of spoken language*: the mechanism is, broadly, that of language acquisition in general. 'Our contention is that acquisition of literacy is an extension of natural language learning for all children . . . we see both oral and written language as learned in the same way' (Goodman, 1982). 'The natural method of learning to read is just the same as that of learning to talk' (Huey). 'Learning to read involves no learning ability that children have not already been called upon to exercise in order to understand the language spoken at home' (Smith).

This is not to claim that what goes on in the child's head is the same for both skills but to suggest that the method of acquisition might usefully be compared. Which begs the question, If reading can be acquired in some ways as speech is, how is speech acquired? Perhaps by something like Huey's 'method of imitation' in which babies are seen as imitating the behaviour of other speakers; by being surrounded by speech; by taking gradually what is meaningful from all the language they are immersed in; by joining in and being supported in what little they can do until they are able to do more. No one 'teaches' a child to talk; the child learns. Says Margaret Meek: 'You encourage him by responding and he learns to talk by talking.' It is, perhaps, the perfect example of true apprenticeship.

But how can this be related to reading? 'The best way to get a reading vocabulary is just the way a child gets his spoken vocabulary, by having the new words keep coming in a context environment that is familiar and interesting and by trying to use them as they will serve his purposes' (Huey). My mother used to describe my daughters' first efforts at conversation as 'talking scribble', and it was pleasant to find this analogy also used by Huey: '. . . [printed language] has, at first, as little meaning as had the spoken sentences, and his scribbling as little like writing or printing as his early babble was like speech.' The theorists seem to be suggesting that reading, like speech, can also be developed by apprenticeship; by a process of support and imitation; by children gradually taking over as more text becomes meaningful. The secret of it all lies in the adults' reading to and with the child as they spoke to and with him while he was learning to talk. 'The steps from this facile* reading and writing are as certain and natural as were the earlier ones for spoken language' (Huey). 'In the same way young fluent readers learn by being invited to become co-readers' (Meek).

The second vital point about the apprenticeship model is that *essentially reading cannot be taught in a formal sequenced way any*

---

*A word that has changed its morality; here Huey means 'easy, fluent'.

more than speech can be. For a long time I had known that the best readers in my classes were those I had taught least to. Despite this awareness I had somehow assumed that the poor readers were like that because they had not had *enough* teaching. Was not a more logical response that they were poor readers because they had had *too much* teaching?

> In such classrooms, there always are two kinds of learners; one kind do well on the skill drills because they have enough control of the reading process . . . They don't need the skill instruction. The second kind have great difficulty with the sequenced skills because they are dealing with them as abstractions . . . such learners can't profit from skill instruction. (Goodman, 1982)

> Children cannot be taught to read. A teacher's responsibility is not to teach children to read but to make it possible for them to learn to read. (Smith)

This explains the many paradoxes with which teachers are so familiar. The children who read from word to word, 'sounding out' just as they have been taught but somehow never making any sense of the text; not understanding or listening to what they read. The child who just seems to know what new words are without ever having been shown how to word build. The child who can work through 'power builders' and 'skill builders' in S.R.A. exercises but doesn't 'get' the point of the passage being worked on. Children who can read a school text with ease but see no point in reading if they don't have to.

Somewhere these children have been taught reading but have failed to learn it. There must be more to reading than the skills that seem to make it up. Like the Tardis, reading is bigger inside than outside; more than the sum of its parts. Maybe it is not the case that children have to learn formal skills of decoding in order to read but that they must learn to read in order to use formal skills.

The third proposition is that *reading is not a series of small skills fluently used; it is a process of getting meaning* and must be so from the start. The most moving account of the importance that meaning has in young children's reading comes in *Teacher*, where Sylvia Ashton-Warner describes 'organic' and 'inorganic' language: the former stems from the child's own needs, emotions and interests, a living, growing form; the latter is imposed on the child from outside and is essentially meaningless to him. The point is emphasized by Goodman (1982): 'We put a book in a six-year-old's hand and say "Here, read it". When he or she can't we say "See, that child can't read". We're ignoring the fact that children can read McDonalds and Burger King and Alpha-bits and Count Chocula and all kinds of things that have meaning for them.'

In other words, children must care about what they are reading. 'The child who is a successful early reader. . . [will] recall, with powerful nostalgia, [his] earliest books; the thrill of Peter Rabbit . . . , the Little Red Engine, the giant turnip, the magic, the mystery and the strange spells that reading wove' (Meek). 'The material that children are asked to read should be closely linked to their own interests and experiences . . . the personal words a child accumulates will depend on his interest' (McKay et al.).

But meaningful reading is more than reading that provokes an emotional response. It also implies text that makes sense, that is written in 'ordinary', connected speech patterns to which the reader can listen as he reads, expecting the next words to link to the previous ones in ways he understands and can predict. Marie Clay describes a child who was discovered to be reading a text down the page in columns, producing 'Go, go, go, go. Tim up. Up Tim. Up, up, up.' Clay considers this to show that the child's concept of the directionality of print is immature – which is true. Read from left to right, however, the text became 'Go Tim. Go up. Go up Tim. Go up, up, up.' It is not, after all, possible to say that the latter version makes any more sense than the former. The child was reading a text that makes equal sense (or non-sense) whether read from top to bottom or left to right. Mightn't this have contributed to his lack of understanding that it matters which way one reads? Similarly, Donald Moyle describes a child who confused 'caravan' with 'Carol' when reading and suggests that she was 'indiscriminately guessing words from their first few letters'. More seriously she was obviously paying absolutely no attention to the sense of the text; it is difficult to imagine a text that would make equal sense whether one read 'caravan' or 'Carol'.

Time and again these aspects of the meaning of the text must be emphasized. Huey describes 'the danger of reading words rather than ideas'. Moira McKenzie says, 'Readers do not just read words, they process language and respond to ideas and feelings.' And again Frank Smith: '. . . rather than the words giving meaning to sentences, it looks as if the sentences are giving meaning to the words', a view echoing almost exactly that of Ronald Morris, who described context-supported, responsive reading right from the start of a child's experience of print.

This need for emotional and structural meaning in what children read seems so unexceptional that it is difficult to credit how little the two aspects of meaningful reading are considered in schools even now. In 1976 Joan Dean was able to advise teachers that 'at an earlier stage [the child] may need to build the word from images of the component sounds before starting on the process leading to meaning', a statement that seems to turn the truth exactly on its head. Similarly, authors like Nora Goddard and even Marie Clay describe a rich and full language-experience pre-reading programme but assume it will lead to a reading scheme, which 'narrows his field of choice to one book which he is expected to read word-perfectly page by page before he can tackle another' (Pat D'Arcy). The D.E.S. report *Education 5 to 9* (1982) found that in the *majority* of schools 'the children spent a good deal of time decoding print with the result that they read mechanically with little understanding of, or interest in, the content'!

If reading must be full of meaning to the child, this leads naturally to the fourth point made so forcefully in the apprenticeship view of reading. *The text offered to the child is crucially important.* It is no longer enough to work a child through a reading scheme, or even several reading schemes, be they never so colour-coded. The logical challenge to the teacher is to provide such a wide range of real books that children will find their own book, which will be meaningful to them; letting them choose which ones they wish to read and letting them find the meaning for themselves.

How, then, is this to be done? How can a child read a text without controlled vocabulary, without flash cards, without a phonic progession. What do we *do*? Here is the fifth aspect of a natural reading programme: *the role of the adult as guiding friend.*

The adult has three parts to play in helping a child learn to read. The first has already been mentioned; the choosing of organic texts to offer the child, for 'if a child is to find himself in reading, a wide range . . . must be presented to him' (Goodman), and allowing the child to choose what he or she needs to read.

The second role for the adult to undertake is very similar to the parent's in helping a child to speak. Many writers describe this process.

'The adult's job is to read with him what both can enjoy, to let him see how the story goes, to help him observe what is there to be read and to tell him what he needs to know when he finds it difficult' (Meek). 'Children have to make sense of reading so teachers must make sure that reading makes sense to children . . . teachers must help children by making reading easy, not by making it difficult' (Smith). 'Many a child cannot remember when reading began, having pored over books and nursery jingles and fairy tales that were read to him until he could read them for himself' (Huey).

The adult first reads all the story while the child cannot read any, then the child will put in the words she or he knows while the adult reads the rest, then the child will take over the reading. All this with a known text first of all, rather as the child learnt to speak a little at a time in forms that were familiar, until finally enough vocabulary is acquired

13

to tackle new text (although still with an adult to help if needed). This, of course, at once negates the idea of books being 'too hard' for a child or the need for any form of colour coding, since the child can behave like a reader whatever the difficulty of the text and the adult will take over whatever the child cannot manage. We do not tell toddlers 'You may not try to say a word of three syllables until you can say all the words with only two.' When a child tries to say 'vegetable' we praise, not prevent – even if the word becomes 'vekble'.

Huey describes a child learning to read like this, 'almost as naturally as the sun shines', moving from listening as father reads, to getting to know where various words and sentences occur on the page, to feeling and saying the right parts of the story or rhyme, to recognizing the exact words. This process of successive approximation requires 'books of good . . . stories and a mother, father or friend who cares enough for children to play this way and read aloud to them . . . the acquisition of power over new reading matter comes naturally this way'.

Moira McKenzie quotes Vygotsky, 'What a child can do in co-operation today, he can do alone tomorrow.'

Margaret Meek says that, 'from first to last the child should be invited to behave like a reader and those who want to help him should assume that he can learn and will learn'. The adult must provide the environment full of reading experience.

But, even harder, especially for a teacher, is the third role of the adult: to withdraw all hint of failure and competition from the reading situation and ensure that children cannot help but succeed. This means that the child should know what to expect when reading, having already had experience of the story, at least at the beginning of learning. Frank Smith says, 'The solution requires that the teacher should read for the children what they cannot read for themselves' and that they should have 'sufficient prior knowledge of what they are expected to read.'

In other words children should know what they are going to read before they read it. This is not the same as teaching the words of the first primer on flash cards so that all are known before the book is tackled. It means letting the children hear where the story is going and why, so that they can predict the sense and the language. Yet, somehow, there is an uncomfortable feeling that this is 'cheating', that children ought to tackle a text cold or they aren't really reading. This is like saying the toddler isn't really speaking when repeating the name of something after us, or chanting a nursery rhyme. It is the firm expectation of what is likely and possible that is built up by this approach. 'Once children know a poem or story it is surprising how quickly they can locate its parts on the printed page and read it' (Huey). Eventually the child will tackle new text, just as the toddler will make new language constructions.

The apprenticeship approach also requires that the adult accept that the child will make mistakes (in fact, *must* make mistakes) and will need time to sort these out and permission to ignore them if they do not matter. Again, some teachers find this exceptionally difficult, until they are reminded of the analogy with speech. 'Language is learned through hearing it, being part of it, and by using it. Parents and teachers tolerate the fact that children's language gradually grows over a period of time. They don't expect it to be "right" from the start' (McKenzie). It is likely that children eager and willing to read for themselves will make 'mistakes' but as Frank Smith says, 'if a mistake makes no difference, what difference does it make?' and if the mistake does make a difference, a child who is expecting to make sense out of reading will want to correct anything affecting that meaning. Says Huey, 'and even if the child substitutes words of his own, provided these express the meaning . . . the reading has been real . . . For reading is always in the nature of translation'. It is the child who does not understand that reading is supposed to make sense who baulks completely or reads 'horse' for 'house' or 'was' for 'saw' without noticing the incongruity. The freedom to make and, if necessary, correct miscues enables children to tackle new text – 'the pupil gets the new word from context, or it is pronounced for him' (Huey). Children will use the skills they have, and the support of the adult, to make sense of the text. 'It is through sense that children learn to read and until they read well enough to make sense of what they are doing someone must help them. They take over gradually while other people help them at the difficult stages' (Smith).

These, then, are the ideas which challenge most of the conventional practices in our schools; reading schemes, vocabulary control, colour coding, phonic drill, reading tests – all are concentrating on the wrong things. They are obsessed with teaching decoding, not with helping children to learn to be readers. This is why schools fail so many children who never discover the joy of reading; this is why children who do discover that joy do so, time and again, 'in spite of' the efforts of the schools.

If the apprenticeship approach is a better way to teach children about reading, it will also become a better way to teach children about learning itself. As Morris says, 'learning to read is one of the first and most important challenges with which the school confronts the child. In meeting that challenge children inevitably become entangled with much that is involved with learning how to learn and with learning to know oneself as a learner.'

The implication is that if we work with children's natural learning methods rather than against them, they cannot help but have a positive view of themselves as learners and as readers. This is our full responsibility, both to children and to books. Accepting that responsibility means that classroom practice must change.

3   Creating the Conditions

To turn the theory of reading through apprenticeship into practice requires a revolution in the classroom. But it is not easy to begin a revolution. When Northborough School undertook this reassessment in 1982 the difficulties seemed formidable. There were no local schools operating an apprenticeship approach to reading, and no one in the school had used anything other than a conventional, largely skills-based programme. We could draw on no previous experience. Nor were the writers I had studied very helpful in the actual translation of theory into classroom practice. Half past two on a wet Friday did not impinge on them.

There were the parents to worry about: their expectation would be that their children would follow the traditional pattern. Previously reception children worked with a pre-reading programme of flash cards and then moved on to a colour-coded range of reading schemes. They worked through these in a strictly prescribed order until they reached light-blue level, when they were offered free choice within their designated colour band. Word-attack skills were taught from the beginning. It was a system that had the virtue of being clear, straightforward and sufficiently near to what the parents themselves remembered as to be completely unexceptionable. However, if we undertook the sort of approach I wanted, I was afraid we would not be able to offer any structure that could be demonstrated. (In the end this proved not to be the case.) The children could read whatever they wished. Furthermore, we no longer proposed to *teach* reading at all in the generally understood manner; I intended that the children should, like Biddy in *Great Expectations*, 'catch it, like a cough'. It all seemed a parents' nightmare.

There were the resources to consider. It was obvious that reading schemes were, with few exceptions, no longer appropriate. Had we sufficient books to use? What about children's own writing? We had *Breakthrough to Literacy* equipment, which was used primarily as a stimulus for writing. No one in the school had used *Breakthrough* right from the start in order for the children to create their own reading material. It would obviously be back to the manual to reassess my approach to this resource.

We already had a language curriculum which, ironically, I had only recently written and which the headteacher and staff had agreed. Now I wanted to abandon that plan; plainly the staff would also need to understand and support, at least in theory, what I was intending to do. It was the fact that my headteacher gave me his wholehearted support – 'I'll carry the can, if need be. Go ahead' – that finally convinced me it could be done. We might finish the first year wishing we had stuck to *One, Two, Three and Away*, but at least we would have tried.

It was in this spirit that I began to attempt to turn theory into practice, first in the reception class at Northborough, by myself, 'feeling' my way into it. Within a term, so successful was the children's response that colleagues in the rest of the school began using the apprenticeship approach with their classes. Two years later we were offering help to and sharing ideas with other schools throughout Cambridgeshire. Now I am at Brewster Avenue School, an infants school that is wholly committed to this approach, from children in the nursery unit onwards.

From our experience this chapter offers, to those readers who are convinced that they too wish to start such a revolution, some practical suggestions about the three interrelated elements of the apprenticeship approach to reading: the reading children do with their own parents or other carers; the books they read; and the teacher's role as guide, assessor, planner and co-ordinator of children's reading behaviour.

Reading at home

Reading at home is the root system that feeds the apprentice reader; if the people at home understand and support what we are doing, everything at school will be made so much easier. If we cannot carry the parents with us, whatever we do will be diminished.

Northborough had long been a school committed to parent involvement; parents came in whenever they wished to help, or to watch, and reading books had always gone home for extra reading practice. This meant that parents expected to be included in their children's education, although never to the extent required by this new approach to reading. It meant that many parents were quite prepared to be highly critical; we had suggested forming a partnership with them, and they were not prepared to be sleeping partners! It was important that they understood our aims. How much more important this understanding is in a school where parents have not enjoyed such a relationship before.

Several studies have emphasized the role of parental influence on reading progress (the Bristol project on preschool language; the Bradford Book Flood report; the Haringey Reading Project; Margaret C. Clarke's *Young Fluent Readers* are only a few). By and large the main emphasis has been on parents 'hearing' children read in the conventional manner. But it is not enough that parents should simply do as they have been done to; instead they should undertake reading to and with their child. It is vital that we explain to all the involved adults what we are doing. Gordon Wells, reporting the Bristol project, says, 'Those families who are succeeding in encouraging their children to talk with skill and fluency can also be shown how to read to them and introduce them to the written language.'

For a small child divided loyalties are destructive and exhausting; we want school and home to be united, each offering a unique contribution to reading development. After all, the home can offer time, individual attention, consistent support and loving concern; the school can offer expertise, suitable texts and understanding of progression. Between the two, the child should thrive.

Approaching the parents. Different schools will have different ways of approaching parents: through formal or informal meetings, home visits, booklets. The main consideration is: What will we tell the parents about this 'new' attitude to reading?

We want them to understand that we intend to learn from them. Parents have helped their children to learn all that they are able to do before school; this has happened through apprenticeship and without formal teaching. It is reassuring to parents to feel that reading can also be learned naturally and that they already know how this can occur.

There is help, though, that the school needs to offer parents and that goes rather beyond the 'pre-reading' advice usually given.

First, we need to do parents the courtesy of considering them as equal partners in the learning process. After all, they can actually be better at reading with children than we are; on the whole they have more time, fewer interruptions and less pressure on them than we, in the classroom, have. Therefore, by contacting every parent, in formal and informal ways, by showing a video of children reading in the classroom, by confirming parents' instinctive knowledge of children's learning patterns, we explain both the school's and the home's role in supporting that learning.

The second approach to parents comes with the actual books themselves. There is no doubt that if this experience-based project is to work, the input of books and print has to be far more than teachers alone can manage; hence the value of the child reading each night at home. Equally, however, the quality of the experience is important and, obviously, when using organic texts the experience gained from

18

each text will be different. Somehow we need to express this to the parents.

It is here that booknotes can help. At the back of each book that the child takes home we stick a small plastic pocket enclosing a card particular to that book. The card suggests some simple activities, word games, questions or discussion points that could be undertaken *if the child wishes*. These are the sorts of activities teachers often undertake in school – we offer them for parents' use as well.

Parents also like a booklet (we call ours *Helping Your Child to Read*; see pages 20 to 26) that outlines reading development: this reminds them about showing their child the print, allowing her or him to pretend to read and, most important, warns them not to force the child's participation. One parent told me she kept her booklet in the kitchen drawer and read it while she got the tea! A booklet certainly seems useful for keeping basic ideas in the forefront of parents' awareness.

All along we intend to offer to parents helping their child to read everything that teachers use when helping their child to read. There is nothing we can do with a book that a parent can't, and how else can children have continuity and security as they work? When teachers say 'Our parents wouldn't help like that', perhaps they mean 'Our parents don't know how to.' Perhaps when parents worry about the school's contribution, *they* feel that *we* don't know how their child has learned for the past four or five years. If we are equal partners, we will share each other's expertise.

The Books

The second element in the apprenticeship approach to reading consists of the books we offer the children when they read with us.

Published texts. There is only one criterion that needs to be taken into account when choosing books for any age of child if reading is to be approached as a natural learning activity. Will the child enjoy the book? There is no need to worry about vocabulary control, type face, phonic consistency or any of the other problems beloved of teachers' manuals. After all, children learn to speak while hearing speech of a wide range of complexity, dialect, volume and meaning. If the adult is to provide support, it matters only that the child should want to read that book.

(continued on page 27)

Pages 20 to 26 reproduce part of Northborough School's booklet for parents, *Helping Your Child to Read*.

The Printed Books

We do not use a reading scheme in the school; your child will not have 'flash cards', 'word tins' or pre-readers; nor will s/he have to work through Book 1, Book 2 and so on.

Instead, we have chosen a very wide range of 'real' story books - just the ones that you will find in the library or bookshop. They have been picked because they are good stories easy to read and remember, with predictable, natural language. These are the sort of books that children love to listen to and soon try to read for themselves.

If you want to buy or borrow books for your child, please do not go for "reading schemes"; we, or your local librarian, will gladly recommend books your child will enjoy. A book club, the See-Saw Club, is run by the school to help your choice and once a month your child will bring home an order form for a wide selection of very reasonably priced books. One book a month will grow into a highly-prized library which will do more than anything else to make your child feel like a real reader. His or her own library ticket is also a great boost.

"a highly prized library...."

Sentence Maker Books

As well as printed books your child will soon be making his or her own story books using a sentence maker. When these little books are finished they will be brought home to keep. Your child will enjoy reading them to you!

If you would like to see sentence maker being used by the children, please ask your child's teacher for an invitation to spend a morning in school so that you can see how these little books are made.

21

What can you do to help?

1. At the beginning

Your child will bring home a "book bag". This will contain a book that your child has chosen and, at the back of the book, some notes for you suggesting approaches to the story.

It is not intended that you should teach your child to read this book; we do not expect him or her to come back to school able to read every word.

Instead, we hope that you will read the story with your child on your lap just as you always do but bearing in mind these points.

- Make sure the child can see the print and pictures.

- Point to the words as you read them.

- Use the pictures as well. There is often additional story in them.

- Allow plenty of time for discussion before you turn over. A valuable question is "What do you think will happen next?".

- Let your child "read" the story to you afterwards - even if this is reciting by heart or making the story up from the pictures. This is a very important stage. Children learn to behave like readers by these activities. Praise all their attempts.

If your child is too tired or reluctant to join in, just make it an opportunity for you to read in a relaxed, enjoyable way. Do not force participation.

When you and your child would like a different book send the book bag back to school for a "refill".

If your child particularly likes a story s/he may want to hear it over and over. This should be encouraged (if you can stand it!). You may find that a very well loved story like this is the first one that your child learns how to read independently.

While you are undertaking these activities at home your child's teacher is doing just the same thing in the classroom. You and she are giving the children the very great experience of meaningful print that will move them nearer and nearer to being readers themselves.

".. bringing home a
book bag..."

23

Later On

After your child has had a lot of books read to him or her and has gained many words in sentence maker work, you may find that his or her behaviour begins to change during story sessions. Now you will find your child beginning to pick out words in the book, reciting the text accurately and trying to match the spoken words with the text by pointing with a finger.

At this point, as you settle for a book session, ask the child, "Shall I read or shall you?". If the child would like to try then let him or her do as much as possible, being ready to help if your child asks you to.

Remembering these points will help.

- <u>Read the story to the child first.</u> This is not "cheating", it is helping him or her to know where the story is going and helps prediction of the text.

- <u>Do not help and correct</u> when the child tries unless the child gets into real difficulties and has obviously lost the sense. Keeping quiet is difficult but children need to learn to puzzle out text from the sense they expect to find.

- Do not worry if the child's reading is not word perfect. If s/he is making sense it does not matter if s/he reads "house" instead of "home" or "Good dog, Spot" instead of "Good boy, Spot".

It would matter, however, if s/he read "he got on his house and rode away". Obviously the sense has been lost and you should offer to take over if your child doesn't want to carry on or if s/he asks you to. Never make him or her feel that s/he must read. This destroys confidence and introduces the idea of testing and failure. Always be ready to read the story yourself if necessary.

At this stage it is helpful to see your child as beginning an apprenticeship in reading. S/he is going to work alongside you, the skilled craftsman; gradually the apprentice can undertake more and more of the task but you will continue to support and guide for as long as you both feel it is necessary.

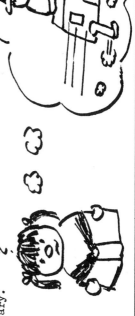

Later Still

As your child's confidence and skill grows you will find s/he reading to you more and more. Bear in mind though that the children have free choice of books and may sometimes choose a book that they cannot yet manage alone. When this happens by all means return to the earlier activities and read to your child. S/he will still need to hear more difficult text than s/he can manage alone.

Remember also all the points on previous pages. It is vital that your child is confident, relaxed and sure s/he can make sense of the story. Don't apply pressure and don't insist on absolute accuracy. The sense is the vital consideration.

".. a book they cannot yet manage alone...."

(continued from page 19)

I developed an informal checklist as an initial sorting procedure when faced with a new book. Basically this involves distinguishing between organic and inorganic texts; between 'wholefood' and 'junk food' books. (Chapter 4 deals more fully with the following points.)

— Can the story, however simple, be read aloud by an adult in a natural, interested manner and without sounding lunatic?

— Is the language natural, predictable, 'sensible' and meaningful?

— Is there some special attribute – humour, pattern, high quality of illustration and colour – that will appeal to children?

— Do text and illustration work together dynamically?

— Most importantly, is the book a real one? That is, one which has been written by a real author who wanted to write a book for children, not a book for teaching reading. (It will be noticed that, by and large, real books have authors; reading schemes have publishers.)

Jill Bennett's *Learning to Read with Picture Books* and *Reaching Out* provide an excellent basic selection for building up natural-reading resources.

This does not need to be an expensive way of beginning reading; although we abandoned our reading-scheme stock, we found that by using the library service we could stock the classroom with books which in many cases were so satisfying to the children that they read them over and over again: several 'reads' for the choosing of one!

Home-made books. Schools should also consider how to offer children the experience of creating their own texts. If children are to understand how to operate on written language, they need a way of demonstrating that understanding. The advantages offered by a *Breakthrough* approach can only enhance the work done with published texts. These advantages are that working with sentence makers shows the transformation of speech into writing actually taking place; it demonstrates dynamically the structure of written language (words as units, left/right progression, sentence structure and simple syntactical rules); and since the text produced is what children want to say, written language is seen as vital and meaningful and has a structure natural to the child. As a result, the child is given power over written language.

27

The alternative model of reading implies that the learner operates on the written language, so a system that actually allows children to do this physically and in the most literal sense is bound to reinforce the child's ability to create meaning for her/himself. In fact, one hears children saying things like, 'Now I'm going to make it say . . . ' or 'I'll change that sentence to make it different' – implying a sense of their own power and a lack of any awe in the presence of written language.

Jesse Reid (in Donaldson, 1983) says that reading readiness 'is not a question of physical, or even mental abilities but is an understanding of what writing is, how it works and what it does'. *Breakthrough* is specifically designed to enable that understanding.

Ronald Morris, describing a context-support model of beginning reading, suggests that 'at first everything is in the mind of the reader before it is encountered in print'. He assumes that the text will be dictated to the teacher by the child. With the sentence-maker books Morris's suggestion of, initially, one hundred percent 'context support' is a reality and, furthermore, the child is not helplessly relying on teacher-as-scribe but from the beginning takes responsibility for creating the text, even if the teacher then fixes it in a book.

The children's home-made books provide their first independent reading material, and because the words they use are such everyday ones, they soon find the same words in published books. After all, if words like 'and', 'is', 'my' or 'can' are truly 'key words', there is absolutely no need to devise books consisting of such words. They will, obviously, occur more frequently than any other in every book.

Seeing children's excitement when they find one of 'their' words in a storybook is a never-failing pleasure. As Tom said to me one day, 'Words in my sentence-maker book belong to me, but words in stories belong to everybody in the world.' What satisfaction there must be in such a thought!

The role of the teacher

If it is true that parents (or any adult) are as effective as, or better than, the teacher at helping a child become a reader; if it is no longer necessary to teach decoding skills *before* children learn how readers behave, if we need no colour coding or reading schemes – what is the teacher to do? How will she know if the child is progressing? Where is the structure?

Reading with the child. Consider the way a teacher works with children to help them learn about reading. The model we take is of the good parent – but there are some differences. The good parent knows how his or her own child learns and develops; the good teacher knows how *all* his or her children learn and develop. This gives a different slant to the teacher's understanding. But nevertheless, just as with the parent, the teacher will read *with* the child, sharing and helping and, above all, enjoying the book. What is involved in reading with the child in this way? There are great differences between 'hearing a child read' and 'reading with a child', differences that may require a change in attitude on the part of the teacher.

Several authors have written about ways of hearing children read, suggesting the most valuable teaching strategies, outlining techniques of miscue analysis, supplying practical and theoretical support for the teacher. (Examples are the work of Kenneth Goodman, Vera Southgate, Elizabeth Goodacre, Marie Clay and Helen Arnold). But, in the main, these authors have assumed that the child will be doing all the reading with the adult in some sense sitting in judgement, noting miscues, giving direct teaching or asking comprehension-testing questions. I have, however, already described the approach we wish to adopt as a craftsman/apprentice relationship in which the adult demonstrates the craft and supports the children in whatever contribution they are able to make. The objective, therefore, is essentially different; we are not listening *to* the child perform, we are performing *with* the child.

This requires some difficult readjustment. The adult is required to let the child decide what she or he can read; the adult must accept that children are not 'cheating' if they read a text already known or if they ask the adult to read first and then follow; that the vital object of the exercise is not to see if the child can decode, build words, guess from context or exercise any other skill, but to get meaning and pleasure from the story.

The nearest approach to this change of emphasis is described by Helen Arnold, who outlined the techniques that could make up a 'shared reading interview', which she suggests would become 'a relaxed and enthusiastic dialogue between teacher and pupil'. Unfortunately, she concludes by saying that 'to propose such complex interaction seems perhaps over-idealistic'. It is, I would suggest, only idealistic if the teacher considers the reading process to be a behaviourist activity. Because reading must be seen as developing in much the way that speech does, 'such complex interaction' is crucial. It is also absolutely vital, of course, that the text is one that will sustain and repay such detailed study.

We also need to consider how without schemes, colour coding or skills teaching we are going to be aware of children's progress.

Recording progress. Teachers worry about progression; they feel, quite rightly, a responsibility to chart and record the progress a child makes. What this usually means, however, is that schools confuse the process of reading development with the process of reading organization; their record sheets and checklists record nothing about the child but only something about how the school organizes that child. What does it tell you about the strategies, understanding or enjoyment a child brings to a book to know that she or he is 'on yellow' or 'on Book Four' or knows fourteen sounds? It may be comforting to know that he or she has 'read' books 1, 1a, 1b, 1c and 2, or is reading at purple level, but does it tell us what the child is actually doing with that book or actually understands about that colour level? We have confused an arbitrary and externally imposed structure with knowing something about reading behaviour; it tells us nothing important. It is also totally against a child's natural learning pattern. We do not say to a child, 'The next word you learn to speak *must* be "cauliflower"', nor do we say some words are 'too easy' or 'too hard' and forbid them to be said; nor do we suppose that testing verb endings will tell us how fluent a child's speech is.

Instead, suppose we substitute the consideration of what actually happens to children when they are allowed to become readers naturally at their own pace in an apprenticeship situation. Is it possible that reading behaviour can be spotted, noted and encouraged in the same way that physical development or oral progress can be? After all, physical skills develop in all normal children in a predictable natural sequence; some develop these faster than others but the progression is the same and it cannot be taught or forced, only encouraged and practised. Does reading development have this same internal structure that supports and indicates the child's progress towards maturity?

I believe it has. And the progress itself provides the structure to support reading through apprenticeship. It is this behaviour development which makes colour coding or reading schemes unnecessary. This is what we have in mind when we are helping children towards reading. What does the child already know about the reading process? What behaviour needs encouragement? What does the child understand?

As children experience more and more of the reading process, they begin to exhibit a variety of behaviours with the texts. (See 'Reading Behaviour Development' outline, page 31.) It does seem that all children, at their own speed, will move through these changes, and they are types of behaviour predicted by virtually all the theorists of this approach, ranging from (at the simplest response) listening passively to (with more complexity) reading with complete independence.

The point that must be made and understood, however, is that the

READING BEHAVIOUR DEVELOPMENT

Adult reads text

Child listens to story – watches pictures.

Child listens to story – observes text.

Child listens to story – vocalizes with adult.

Child offers to read some or all of text at any level below.

Child's behaviour with known text

Child 'makes up' story – no pointing, word match or even accurate recall. May not even seem to look at print.

Child 'tells' story – accurate retelling, no pointing or word match. Aware of the text.

Child tells story with finger. Accurate retelling of story, runs finger along lines, often matches beginning and ending of line with voice and finger.

Child tells story with word/sound match. Tells accurately, complete word-by-word voice match. Very fluent.

Child's behaviour with unknown text

Child reads known words. A mixture of reading and telling. Child may comment, 'I've got that word in my sentence maker.' Unknown words may be made up entirely, using no clue other than general sense. Child's finger often stabs at known words, slides over unknown. Still very fluent.

Child reads known words; uses context, phonic clues, general configuration to decode unknown ones. Decoding often inaccurate, e.g., 'house' for 'home'. Reading may slow down to word-by-word rate.

Child reads known words, decodes unknown ones with accuracy, using context, phonics, and so on. Unknown words are far fewer and tackled with confidence. Reading may be basically fluent, slowing down at 'tricky bits'.

Note about Reading Behaviour Development outline. No child is at only one stage at one time. Although the levels are generally hierarchical, there isn't a time pattern. A child may display several types of behaviour, even when reading one book. The skills exhibited by the child depend on the text being read rather than on the child's ability. Complex text will tend to encourage earlier skills; simpler text can be read with more complex skills.

level of the child's response depends not on the child's maturity, ability, experience or age but *on the text they are involved with.*

This is the understanding behind the development of reading behaviour outlined here to provide the teacher with a structure to support the apprenticeship approach. It *is* important to be able to say what a particular child has achieved, what progress he or she is making. We do this by noting each strategy a child brings to reading, each sign of increasing maturity. The teacher must be sensitive to the child, ready to support and encourage first attempts, ready to help the child practise developing abilities. It may be more demanding than merely noting what book or phonic blend the child has 'done', but it is infinitely more rewarding.

We cannot make a child show any of these strategies, any more than we can make a child able to walk; these abilities can only come from within the child. Our privilege, as the skilled practitioners, is to offer to the learner the encouragement and conditions that enable the activities and then to allow the child to practise them in safety until they are truly 'second nature' – just as walking is. We are all fluent walkers, but we were not taught to walk; we learnt how to walk. Fluent readers develop in the same way, if we allow them to.

This premise has implications for assessment, testing, even for simple recordkeeping. What it suggests is that any one child may show several different kinds of behaviour depending on what is being read, or even several different kinds of behaviour within one book. Thus a child who will need to listen passively while *Owl at Home* is read will read independently perhaps six or seven words of *Bears in the Night* and will exhibit highly sophisticated, independent decoding ability when reading *Humpty Dumpty* or, in a home-made book, *My Brother is little I love him.* Similarly, one child may say 'You read this' when bringing *Little Bear's Friend*, listen while getting into the story, say 'I can read this bit,' ask for help, listen again and finish by saying 'Now I'll read the end.' There may be three or four different reading behaviours and levels of response within one ten-minute period with one text.

Learning to read is a not a straightforward movement through time, one skill piled on another, one behaviour built on the first. And yet we have acted as if it is. We have lost the natural ebb and flow – we have literally forced children into unnatural behaviour, making them always drive forward or fail.

When the teacher is reading with a child, it is important to have the outline of the natural development of reading behaviour in mind. When a child shows some behaviour for the first time, it can be noted down; when the behaviour has become part of the child's usual strategy, it can be coloured in on the wheel record sheet (see page 33), which has been devised in a circular fashion to avoid an impression of

READING EXPERIENCE RECORD FOR A PRIMARY SCHOOL.

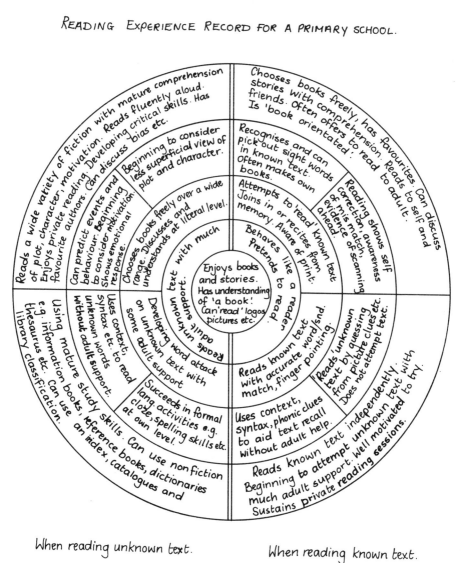

When reading unknown text.   When reading known text.

This wheel covers children's development from pre-school to the end of the primary school. We found it helpful to shade in by colour, thus: red, ages four to six; blue, ages six to eight; and green for eight upwards. This helped to show periods of rapid progress or plateaux in development.

The same sort of reading behaviour is covered several times at different levels of maturity since, for example, prediction techniques are present from the beginning at a very simple level and are still developing in the fluent reader.

The brief synopsis of each behaviour on the chart should, of course, be expanded in the school's language document.

straight-line development. This gives an immediate visual impression of what a child can and can't do with published or home-made text at all levels of difficulty.

This is the structure which natural reading has and which, at their own pace, children will develop as they learn to be readers. It is the teacher's job to be aware of each child's progress on these lines and to guide, encourage, plan and note each child's progress towards reading maturity.

It is not necessary, in fact it is counterproductive, to control the books the children read, the words they use or the speed they progress at. The hardest change for teachers to make in their attitudes is this 'letting go' of control over the child's progress. We *cannot* control it. But how difficult it is to admit this; in my first term of using the apprenticeship approach, round about October, just before the first children 'broke through' to reading, I lost my nerve and tried to make some of them read *Link-up 1* to see if they could be said to be 'on a colour level' yet. It failed. And serve me right. But how hard the old habits die!

Conventionally we have taught children the skills of decoding and hoped they would become readers. How much better to make them into readers and then help the skills to develop – as they will, with children's increasing understanding of the purpose of reading and the pleasure it gives.

4   Real Books for Real Readers

Books are an end in themselves: they are the reason for reading, not merely the objects by which people are enabled to learn to read. We are hoping to offer the world of literature to children; to show even the youngest, least mature beginner in books that within the covers of a loved book is an adventure of the spirit – something that can speak to that child alone and lead her or him into a wider world.

We often tend not to ask why children should learn to read and behave as though the learning is sufficient in itself. It is because we have not offered enough purpose to the learning that we fail to capture so many children. Wisely chosen books provide the purpose; we learn to read in order to make this world our own.

The medium and the message are, in fact, inseparable; children cannot receive the message that books are joyous and meaningful from dreary, meaningless books. We offer impoverished texts and wonder that many children do not much want to read them or that, if they do, they read to please us, or their parents, or for the kudos of finishing another book. These motives are unlikely to sustain a love of reading through school days and into adulthood.

The books, then. At this point it is useful to borrow Sylvia Ashton-Warner's distinction between organic and inorganic teaching. A similar distinction applies to books; an organic book has grown from the author's desire to write that particular story in that particular way: it is a natural, wholefood approach to writing. The opposite is a book that has been written only to teach reading – it has no life of its own. Such a book is manufactured from additives labelled 'phonic approach' or 'controlled vocabulary' and preservatives labelled 'a complete language programme for your school' or 'a complete introduction to vital skills'. The junk food of the print world.

'When one considers that most children have a spoken vocabulary of 2000 to 3000 words at the age of five it is obvious that a reading vocabulary of 50 to 100 words taking sometimes weeks to get through is likely to be not only boring but to contain very few of the words they really want to use' (Leslie Webb, 1969). Margaret Meek asserts that 'Literature makes readers in a way that reading schemes never can.' Huey describes the child's reaction to real books, 'Now the child . . . loves a story, loves to get somewhither in what is said, wants an outcome to the discussion, and has a persistence and continuity of thought that are constantly violated by such "sentence-hash" [in primers]'.

If we intend children to behave like readers right from the start, they must be allowed to develop the strategies of real readers. How can they use prediction, context clues, grammatical and meaningful guesses on arbitrary, isolated words and exhortations? Sarah, who read 'Here is Pat the dog', and then asked 'Why?' was asking more than she knew.

The teacher's responsibility, therefore, is very great: to offer a wide variety of organic texts, whether published or the child's own, and then to help the child read whatever he or she wishes to. This is how the real meaning and purpose of those black marks on the page are unfolded to the child.

The first quality a real book will possess is a very practical one, it reads aloud well. This is probably the easiest test for any book. Read it aloud; if it interests you and reads well it will be worth reading to the children. If they enjoy it, put it on the shelves. The book has passed the first test; it is entertaining and sounds right.

The second quality is that, however simple, the text must have natural language rhythms, the flow of a true story and furthermore must interest both the child and the adult. (If the teacher cannot stand the book, it will be impossible to share it successfully with a child.) This criterion, of course, precludes books of the 'Come, Lad, come, oh, look' genre, which cannot be read aloud in any sort of natural narrative style. There is no connection between each unit, the next word is quite arbitrary within wide limits; what meaning there is has to be imposed upon the text. There is no narrative flow, no normal grammatical shape. In order to read such books aloud to a class, the teacher would be forced to impose all the missing structure, and it is seldom indeed that such an effort would be worthwhile for the pleasures of the plot!

In itself, sparse text does not help the beginning reader if simplicity is confused with paucity. If all normal linguistic cues and clues are removed, the reader has a far harder struggle to make sense of the writing; it also allows the misconception to develop that reading is just a matter of getting individual words right rather than of getting meaning from those words.

Brian Wildsmith's *The Island* uses only fifteen words; they have a narrative shape, are easy to speak ('Look, there's an island!'), relate a cheerful joke (even, to very small children, a real surprise), and there is a nice pun on the last page to amuse the adult. It reads aloud well and is simple in a childlike way; hence, probably, its great popularity with children.

In many organic books of this sort an inevitability in the language enables the reader to be 90% right about the text even if the words are totally unknown. Amanda, who had no sight vocabulary at all, had never heard the story of *Not Now, Bernard* by David McKee (but knew its title), 'read' me the story of the first two pages like this: 'Bernard says hallo to daddy, his daddy said "Oh, not now Bernard".' The actual text was '"Hallo dad", said Bernard. "Not now Bernard," said his father.' Her match was even closer further on; in fact she 'read' exactly what was on the page. 'Bernard went into the garden."Hallo, monster," he said to the monster. The monster ate Bernard up.' That is inevitability – a frequent attribute in organic texts and proof of natural, predictable language.

Inevitability also arises out of the third quality of a real book: the close match between text and illustration and the genuine commitment of the artist to the story. It can be no accident that so many of the books which beginning readers love and succeed with come from artist-authors. John Burningham, Pat Hutchins, Maurice Sendak, Brian Wildsmith, and Quentin Blake are all writers who are also their own illustrators. In most cases this results in beautiful, witty, meaningful illustrations that are so closely linked to the text it is almost as though the words have grown out of the pictures. The two forms work together to create the totality of meaning.

36

This is not the same process as is frequently seen in the 'pre-readers' of a reading scheme. There the words are either simply labels, as in caption books, which advance the meaning of the book not one whit, or they are arbitrary selections from all the possible words suggested by the picture and are simply imposed upon it. This is very common, especially in the first two or three levels of schemes where the pictures are full of incident or detail (to encourage 'language development skills') and the print says merely 'Look' or 'Peter is here' or 'a big shop and a little shop'.

Instead, consider the story of *Titch* by Pat Hutchins, in which a little boy, constantly derided and belittled by his older and bigger brother and sister, finally achieves something greater than either of them. Here the words and pictures constantly enhance and extend each other. The inevitable, simple text is deepened and extended by the expressions on the characters' faces, and the clear uncluttered pictures are defined and explained by the words. Many a younger brother or sister has identified with Titch. When I asked Darren, youngest of three, how Titch feels, he said, 'Like a bit left over.' He read the book four times in one sitting and then took it home, saying, 'I'm going to read this to Tracey, very loudly!'

Often the sheer merit of the pictures, as in Pat Hutchins's *Goodnight, Owl!* or Maurice Sendak's *Where the Wild Things Are*, intrigues children and leads them to want to know the book.

What other qualities will increase the chances of choosing a book that inspires both love and reading? Look in the text for humour, tension, pattern, rhythm or familiarity.

Spooky books or surprising books are natural magnets. They appeal to children so strongly that they are often read over and over again for the intense pleasure and satisfaction they provide. Examples of this sort of book are legion. *The Spooky Old Tree* and *Bears in the Night* by the Berenstains; *Creepy Castle* by John Goodall; *Where's Spot?* by Eric Hill; *Where the Wild Things Are* by Maurice Sendak and *The Fat Cat* by Jack Kent are only a few of the surprising or spooky books which children enjoy.

Funny books are equally loved. *Mr Magnolia* by Quentin Blake, David McKee's *Not Now, Bernard*, Marilyn Sadler's *It's Not Easy Being a Bunny*, and several of the Read Together books from Story Chest have had children beaming with laughter.

Pattern and rhythm have two functions. First, children respond to them emotionally; second, they make a book easier to read. Strong pattern will carry young readers through a book when they could not actually tackle a text of such complexity without it. Pattern encourages prediction, phrasing, word recognition, and it gives the same security as nursery rhymes or skipping songs. Stories like the Ahlbergs' *Each Peach Pear Plum*, *The Elephant and the Bad Baby* by Elfrida Vipont and Raymond Briggs, Paul Galdone's *What's in Fox's Sack?*, and *Chicken Soup with Rice* by Maurice Sendak have this irresistible quality which carries the reader along. Children actually *sing* the words of *Chicken Soup with Rice*.

Familiarity is, of course, a valuable attribute of a story. Children are often amazed and delighted to find a nursery rhyme or a folk tale that they know, or have seen on television, in a book. It is a great help to the reader to know what's going to happen, and familiarity also confirms the idea of books as secure friends. The criterion of artistic quality is important, of course. There are many poorly illustrated and designed versions of traditional stories, but there are also many caring, beautiful ones. Helen Oxenbury, Paul Galdone, William Stobbs, among others, have added their own qualities to traditional, timeless texts.

In the end, of course, the final arbiters of the books they need and want are the children themselves. If children love a book, they will want to read it. As Hayley said, 'I'm going to read every story in the library and then get the nicest ones and read them again.' It is our responsibility to choose wisely the books we offer, but we cannot choose the relationship between book and reader. Some books will 'work' for nearly all children (and one or two really do seem to work for *all* children, such as *Each Peach Pear Plum*); some books are neglected by all save two or three. This is why a wide selection and much freedom are essential if the apprenticeship approach to reading is to succeed.

By offering books with these qualities, reading them lovingly and often with the children, and helping each child to read the books that have personal meaning for him or her, we will allow everyone to feel, like Stuart speaking of *Frog and Toad*, that 'I want to read this one again all by myself 'cos I *like* it.'

As Jill Bennett says, 'The books we offer to children transmit the message about what reading is.' Organic books transmit the message that reading is good, satisfying, life-enhancing.

SOME FAVOURITE PICTURE BOOKS

Janet & Allan Ahlberg:
    The Brick Street Boys series (Collins/Picture Lion)
    Each Peach Pear Plum (Kestrel/Picture Lion)
    Funnybones (Heinemann/Picture Lion)
    Happy Families series (Kestrel/Puffin)
    Peepo! (Kestrel/Puffin)

Stan & Jan Berenstain:
    Bears in the Night (Collins, hardback and paperback)
    The Spooky Old Tree (Collins, hardback and paperback)

Quentin Blake: *Mr Magnolia* (Cape/Picture Lion)

John Burningham:
  Mr Gumpy's Outing (Cape/Picture Puffin)
  Mr Gumpy's Motor Car (Cape/Picture Puffin)

Ben Butterworth:
  The Roundabout books (Arnold)
  The Trog books (Wheaton)

Eric Carle: *The Very Hungry Caterpillar* (Hamish Hamilton/Picture Puffin)

P.D. Eastman:
  Go Dog Go! (Collins)
  Are You My Mother? (Collins)

Paul Galdone: *What's in Fox's Sack?* (World's Work)

Sarah Garland: *Going Shopping* (Bodley Head/Picture Puffin)

Mirra Ginsburg: *Good Morning, Chick* (Julia MacRae/Carousel)

John Goodall:*Creepy Castle* and *Shrewbettina's Birthday* (both
  Macmillan/Picturemac)

Susanna Gretz: *Teddybears 1 to 10* (Benn/Picture Lion)

Eric Hill: *Where's Spot?* (Heinemann/Picture Puffin)

Pat Hutchins:
  Good-night, Owl! (Bodley Head/Picture Puffin)
  1 Hunter (Bodley Head/Picture Puffin)
  Rosie's Walk (Bodley Head/Picture Puffin)
  Titch (Bodley Head/Picture Puffin)

Jack Kent: *The Fat Cat* (Picture Puffin)

Judith Kerr:
  Mog and the Baby (Collins/Picture Lion)
  The Tiger Who Came to Tea (Collins/Picture Lion)

Arnold Lobel:
  Owl at Home (World's Work, hardback & paperback)
  Frog and Toad Together (World's Work/Young Puffin)

David McKee: *Not Now, Bernard* (Andersen/Sparrow)

Ron Maris: *My Book* (Julia MacRae)

Else Holmelund Minarik & Maurice Sendak:
  Little Bear, *Little Bear's Visit* and *Friend* (World's Work)

Cliff Moon: *Once upon a Time* series (Ginn)

Helen Oxenbury: *The Enormous Turnip* (Heinemann/Piccolo)

Helen Piers:
Mouse Looks for a House and *a Friend* (Methuen)
Hullabaloo for Owl! (Methuen)

Marilyn Sadler: *It's Not Easy Being a Bunny* (Collins, hardback and paperback)

Maurice Sendak:
Chicken Soup with Rice in *Nutshell Library* (Collins)
Where the Wild Things Are (Bodley Head/Puffin)

Dr Seuss: *Green Eggs and Ham* (Collins, hardback & paperback)

Elfrida Vipont and Raymond Briggs:
The Elephant and the Bad Baby (Hamish Hamilton/Picture Puffin)

Shigeo Watanabe & Yasuo Ohtomo:
How Do I Put It On? (Bodley Head/Picture Puffin)
I Can Build a House! (Bodley Head/Picture Puffin)

Brian Wildsmith:
Cat on the Mat, All Fall Down, The Island (all Oxford Univ. Press)

Charlotte Zolotow & Maurice Sendak:
Mr Rabbit and the Lovely Present (Bodley Head/Picture Puffin)

5 Read with Me

This chapter describes my classroom. I teach 29 infants and, obviously, older children will need some different treatment (they may not really *want* to sit on your lap!). Schools organize their days differently; they may not, sadly, have parent helpers; they may have mixed age groups who can help each other. But whenever teachers talk to me, they ask 'How do you organize your day for this approach?' and it is this question this chapter will answer. But it remains a purely personal answer; each teacher will have personal answers too; nothing here is prescriptive or definitive. Next year may see a different pattern.

If we wish to help children to learn by apprenticeship, we have already seen that we need to consider three elements of experience: the parents', the child's, and the teacher's role.

How is this to be organized? The pattern of the day is a flexible thing – how we start may not be how we finish. But, in general, once the children are settled into school and know me, the day runs like this.

When the children begin arriving, mothers and fathers stay to read a story, or admire a picture until register time. (I have seriously considered providing coffee and a kettle for this period, it seems so pleasant.) The children put their book bags – named plastic bags for taking the books home – in the box for attention later. We talk. Then the business of the day begins: a quota of work for each group, individual or group maths, sentence maker, painting or cutting out, tracing, handwriting practice. Each day a selection of 'formal' work to be done when a child wishes; the rest of the morning is the child's own, to write, to read, to talk. I am available to help, every day a group has direct teaching, depending on what is needed by them. The book corner in the morning is often in the hands of a parent helper; she reads to, with and alongside any child who wishes, just as she does with her own child at home. She also keeps a helping eye available for those who want to read to themselves or to friends.

By lunch time the children have completed their quota and anything else that needs doing to continue a project or begin a new one.

The afternoon is my book corner time. A parent often helps to supervise the rest of the class; they may do anything that does not require direct teaching; in other words, anything that the children can do by themselves or with only a little help that any friendly adult can give. They can practise doing sums they have met; they cannot learn a new set. They can use their present sentence-maker constructions but not learn a new one. Painting, sand, water is worked at. This is the time when birthday cards for mummy are made, when stories for little sister are written, when they sit on the steps and watch the builders laying new tarmac. Between reading sessions I go and join them for a chat.

I am based in the book corner. At first any child who wanted could come to read with me. But this became unmanageable, everybody wanted a turn, so rather reluctantly I was forced to call a group a day; 'Today is red group's reading day'. Each child comes to choose a book, published or home-made, up on my lap, 'Shall I read or shall you?', then the story begins.

We talk about it, predict, look at the words and take our time. I watch, assess, plan and encourage each step the child takes. I can just manage ten minutes or so each. At first, that is long enough for me to read *The Spooky Old Tree* or *Each Peach Pear Plum*. Later, however, we have to split a book, 'more tomorrow', perhaps have only one chapter of *Little Bear's Friend* or half of *Go, Dog, Go*. The difference is that I can read faster than they, and now they want to read. So we often stay in at lunch time, I and three or four children who want to finish a story or who, despite my best intentions, I couldn't fit in yesterday.

This reading with me is the core of the approach and its greatest pleasure. My invitation to the child is 'Come and read with me'; that single word change, from the conventional 'Read *to* me', encapuslates the 'feel' of what we are doing. As a colleague said, 'Once I started saying that, I felt the whole atmosphere lighten and improve.' Even more delightful is to hear the children saying it to me and to each other.

The little children sit on my lap when they read with me so that they are offered literally physical support, are relaxed and comfortable and can see and follow all the text. They are allowed to bring any book they choose, however 'easy' or 'hard', and at first I read it all to them. Later, with some books the children read a little, and later yet a child may read it all. But still, throughout the years, the book and the support are one unit. There is no control other than the child's wishes as to how much or how little is read; if someone wants to read the same book with me every day for a week (and many do), I grin and bear it, for here is a book that is speaking to that child. Later, I ask children 'Will you read, or shall I?' and respect their decision even when it disappoints me. Who is this reading *for* anyway, the teacher or the child?

The final job of the day is for those children who wish to to change their book-bag book to take home. Sometimes they choose to take home a book we have read together, sometimes a new one. The choice is theirs. I record the book the child has chosen on the good old

cardboard 'bookmarker' with the child's name on top. (This recording is not so much for my information – the children always know which books they have had experience of – as for the children's pleasure: they love to see the list of books growing.) I think we are basically running a library!

There are also various reading activities which I encourage but on a more ad hoc basis; they are frequently child-instigated. Examples are the free use of my big sentence maker by the children; the very frequent use of the book corner throughout the day by individuals or groups to read to themselves or their friends, to rest, to browse, to potter; the public reading session, when one or two children volunteer to read a story to the class (especially valuable for the development of a sense of audience and drama). Sometimes they read from a published text, sometimes from their sentence-maker or other home-made books, which – once they are finished and 'bound' with tackyback – are added to the bookshelves along with the published books. Children enjoy reading each other's work, and it is great motivation for the writers. As Kerry said, 'It's good being an author – everyone likes books.'

Another popular activity is group reading. Five or six children love to take turns reading books like the Meg and Mog stories or *Frog and Toad*. They dramatize, discuss, share jokes and argue about the plot. They help each other, suggest possible interpretations and share the reading, perhaps a page each. For older children this approach allows each child to share a longer text, like *The Iron Man* or *The Magic Finger*, before they have the stamina to tackle it alone. It is also a great

43

pleasure for me to preside over these cheerful intellectual forums.

Perhaps unusually with infants, I also deliberately instigate two or three fifteen-minute 'quiet reading sessions' during the week. In these periods we all read (or 'read') together, to ourselves, a book we are interested in. (I use 'we' since I too take a book and join the group.) These periods have several advantages: they throw the children on their own resources and encourage them to puzzle out text without an adult; they show reading as something that can give private pleasure (a discovery many children never make); it is reading in an adult sense (few adults read aloud to other adults) and encourages a mature attitude to what reading is. If we have time, I ask one or two children to report to the rest of the class on what they have been reading.

An excellent discussion of private reading and its value with older children comes in Vera Southgate's *Extending Beginning Reading*, and I was influenced in attempting this activity by that study. However, I am, even so, surprised by the pleasure and maturity even such young children show in this situation. Probably because the books are worthwhile, even if the child is looking only at the pictures, and because the children assume that they are readers and know how to behave like readers, even a group of reception infants can sustain 'private reading' with great confidence. In many ways it is here where the adult is *not* encouraging and supporting that the success of this approach is demonstrated; in the truest sense there are no non-readers; no child fails to show interaction with a book.

The children, of course, are reading throughout the day; they may only have two planned sessions on my knee each week but reading (and its reflection, writing) goes on in many different forms. We have a post office; the children write letters to each other, the staff, their parents. The sentence makers are always present; there is always a child or two working on a 'story' or a book. Once literacy becomes taken for granted it never has to be forced into use. The book corner is never empty.

What do the parents think of all this?

Not one parent fails to support us, or to read regularly with their children. They come into school to see the books and talk about the ones their child loves most. No one asks, 'When will he get a reading book?' or 'Why can't she read yet?' Whether their child is mature or immature in her/his response, the parent sees and feels the confidence and pleasure in books the child feels. Many express surprise at and delight in the speed and fluency of the child's reading. It is as if the parents know too that this is how reading ought to happen; as if parents' anxiety in a conventional situation is a result of their sensing that we are forcing children into unnatural behaviour. Let reading grow, and the parents can relax too. They are wiser than we think. But then they not only see their child's progress, they create most of it; so they should be pleased. How much they enjoy taking part. 'I love to read to her', 'We enjoy it very much', 'We fight over whose turn to read it is', 'Please let her bring *The Elephant and the Bad Baby* again. We enjoyed it so much'. 'Please help him to find a different book – we can't stand *The Hungry Giant* again!' It all gives a new meaning to parental involvement.

And what about the children? How positively do they react? They all believe they are readers. 'Read this with me,' they say or, increasingly, 'Let me read to you.' Right from the beginning books are things they know about and are easy with; reading is not something they will do 'one day' but something they do now – at whatever level. They all, however mature or immature, believe themselves to be readers and behave like readers. Helping them, reading to them first, does not make them lazy. It increases the drive to try for themselves because it increases their confidence and removes the fear of failure.

They love books too. Most experience over a hundred books in a year, and have loved some, discarded others. Those who are reading, to whatever extent, independently made the step with one book that seemed to help them to break through to the next stage. These break-through books vary from child to child, but all have the same characteristic: the child cares enough about the text to be determined to make it his or her own. It does not matter about sentence length, size of print, typeface or any of the other details teachers' manuals are so dogmatic about. All that matters is that the child wants to read the story. The drive is the child's. (As Ashton-Warner says, 'There's no driving to it. I don't teach at all.') I provide the lap, the text and the time; the learning is the child's.

The role of the sentence maker, of their own language, is vital. Here in their own stories are the words children have absolute power over. They have learnt so much by using it: the relationship between speech and print, the word as a unit, the way sentences work; how to say what they want to say. Even more, the children feel in control of written language: it is their own, what shall they make it do?

Children do not fail to read back their text days, even weeks, after it has been composed. They read their books to me, to parents, to anyone who comes in. 'Do you want to draw a picture about your story?' 'No, I've written it.'

By January of their first year the most mature children have taken over completely; they write their own books – 'The Owl Book', 'The Witch and Glenna', 'Mummy's Book', 'A Book about I love Mummy'. Why should they be interested in 'Simon and Elizabeth's mummy' or 'Miss King' when they have a real, important mummy or teacher of their own they can read about?

Many of the words they use with their sentence maker crop up in the published texts too. 'I've got "little" in my sentence maker', 'Look, there's "baby'", or "'school'" or "'naughty'". It must help their response to books.

And how they respond to books!

This is Hannah, aged four, who brought *Fat Cat* to me for four days running, each day needing less help. 'I'll read it all tomorrow,' she said. And did. What a Friday!

There is Mrs Smith, who bought *Creepy Castle* because Daniel loved it so much and also bought *Shrewbettina's Birthday* while she was in the bookshop: 'I knew he'd like it.'

Next is Daniel himself, walking round clutching *Spooky Old Tree* (his break-through book, the one that he first read), reading it to all his friends and, when they tired, reading it to his old comforter, Snoopy.

Simon, reading *If You Meet a Dragon* in assembly – Eric Morecambe's timing could not have been better, building to the climax, pausing before the denouement.

Cathy, crying as she read 'Mother Bear's Robin' with me. 'It was kind of her to let it go, but she loved it a lot, didn't she, to be so sad?'

Colin calling to David, 'There's a good bit here, listen,' and reading the passage where the big red ball is kicked over the wall, 'and that was the end of the big red ball', and shutting the book with a satisfied smack. 'It served him right.'

James has got very assertive these days. He knocks my hand away as we open *In a Dark, Dark Wood*. 'No, me,' he says. 'I can.'

Heidi is listening to *Good-Night, Owl!* (she loves all the noises). Triumphantly, on every page she chants, 'and owl *tried* to sleep'. Her finger charts the words, her voice mirrors Owl's exasperation perfectly. I suppose I know that she is 'only' memorizing, but Heidi knows she's reading: reading is the page coming alive, and it certainly does that for her.

A little boy, referred to the nursery for a special-needs place, had never spoken in his life. Then, every day for three days running, he brought *Each Peach Pear Plum* to his teacher, silently listening as she read it to him. On the fourth day he recited it to her. His first words! The power of a loved book . . .

No classroom using this approach to beginning reading will ever be quite the same again. However the day is organized, whatever the age and ability of the children, if we reach out for the parents, the child and the books and bring them together, we are improving the quality of life – ours and theirs – as well as the quality of our teaching.

POSTSCRIPT

All this – the parents' reaction, the children's progress – is greatly satisfying, but for me and the school the most important discovery of all is that the theory does actually work in practice: for all the children we work with. Fluent eleven-year-olds with reading ages of fifteen and ambitious parents have begun to read books for fun, the demand that they be 'stretched' (like some form of educational elastic) has ceased. They can rest, if they wish, by choosing a silly, 'easy' book or by asking an adult to read *to* them for a while; there is no sense of shame anymore in a retreat. Paradoxically, they read more as a result.

Children of eight or nine, classed once as 'failed' or 'remedial' readers, can no longer fail. Many have had satisfying experiences with books for the first time in their lives; they have discovered that reading books is good and that they *can* do it. Colleagues have watched these children blossom and thrive as they find that reading is not about phonic drill, flash cards or yet another 'remedial scheme' but is about real books and listening to and having a try at a proper story.

Top infants of six discuss the merits of different books as seriously as any panel of radio critics, recommending favourites for a friend to try. 'You'll like *Cat on the Mat*, you have to *spit* when you read it!'

When we offer children the freedom to do what they can with whatever they wish to read, the measure of progress is not that they become able to do what they could not do before but that they become able to apply their abilities to increasingly complex text. All reception children are able to read fluently – it may be only their name, perhaps, or the McDonald's logo on a plastic cup. *At the same time* all reception children are unable to read some things at all; many books are quite beyond even the most mature. Again, the analogy with speech may be drawn – the toddler can say the word 'mummy', needs help with 'chocolate' and cannot manage 'cement mixer'. But adults accept what the child can do, help when he nearly can, and take over when he can't. This is how natural learning takes place in speech, in physical skills, and this is how learning to read takes place. Within two terms, some children can apply *independent* reading behaviours to texts as complex as *The Elephant and the Bad Baby* or *The Fat Cat* or *Father Bear Comes Home*. Others do so with *Bears in the Night*, *Where's Spot?* or *Jack and Jill*. Still a few manage 'only' their sentence-maker books or *Creepy Castle*. But all can read something. All believe they can read.

This response from children is the greatest success of the apprenticeship approach to reading and its greatest justification. Teachers who are now committed to what is still, in many eyes, a revolutionary idea have a responsibility to share experience: to report honestly, to explain clearly, to attempt to face problems conscientiously. Above all, we have the responsibility to express the firm belief that this is the better way to teach children about reading, about literacy, about books, about learning itself.

I believe that the potential for this approach to learning has hardly begun to be explored. Is the reading behaviour development true for all children? What about approaching writing like this? Or maths? What else can parents teach us? The possibilities are great, and like teaching itself, endlessly exciting.

BOOKS FOR FURTHER READING

Helen Arnold: *Listening to Children Reading* (Hodder & Stoughton, 1982)

Sylvia Ashton-Warner: *Teacher* (1963; Virago, 1983)

Jill Bennett: *Learning to Read with Picture Books* (Thimble Press, 1982)

Jill Bennett: *Reaching Out: Stories for Readers of 6 to 8* (Thimble Press, 1983)

Margaret C. Clarke: *Young Fluent Readers* (Heinemann, 1976)

Marie Clay: *Reading* (Heinemann, 1972)

Pat D'Arcy: *Reading for Meaning 1* (Hutchinson, 1973)

Department of Education and Science: *Education 5 to 9* (H.M.S.O., 1982)

Margaret Donaldson: *Development and Education* (Blackwell, 1983)

Nora Goddard: *Literacy: Language-Experience Approaches* (Macmillan, 1974)

Kenneth Goodman: *Language and Literacy I, II* (Routledge, 1982)

Kenneth Goodman: 'Reading – a Psycholinguistic Guessing Game' in *Journal of the Reading Specialist*, May 1967.

John Holt: *How Children Learn* (Penguin, 1967)

Edmund Huey: *The Psychology and Pedagogy of Reading* (1908; Massachusetts Institute of Technology Press, 1972)

David MacKay, Brian Thompson, Elizabeth Shaub: *Breakthrough to Literacy* (Longman, 1970)

Margaret Meek: *Learning to Read* (Bodley Head, 1982)

Moira McKenzie: *Learning to Read and Reading* (Inner London Education Authority, 1979)

Ronald Morris: *Success and Failure in Learning to Read* (Oldbourne, 1963)

Frank Smith: *Reading* (Cambridge University Press, 1978)

Frank Smith: *Understanding Reading* (Holt, Rinehart & Winston, 1978)

Vera Southgate: *Extending Beginning Reading* (Heinemann, 1981)

Leslie Webb: *Modern Practice in the Infant School* (Blackwell, 1969)

Gordon Wells: *Language Development in the Pre-School Years* (Cambridge University Press, 1984)

The Cost of a Child

A report on the financial cost of child-rearing in Ireland

Claire Carney,
Eithne Fitzgerald,
Gabriel Kiely
inn

© Combat Poverty Agency 1994
ISBN 1 871643 33 3
Research Report Series No. 17

The views expressed in this report
are the authors', and are not necessarily
those of the Combat Poverty Agency.

Design and Production
Language *visual communication*